After

HERE ◆to◆ THERE

Getting From CROSS to Your Mission Field

CROSS.Propempo.com

*God in His sovereign providence made this book possible
in the weaving of life's tapestry through study,
ministry experience, relationships, and opportunity.
The Lord used many people to especially encourage
and help this project along, most of all,
my wife, Kathy, but also including Clint Moore,
Mike Pollard, and John Crotts.*

*I am also indebted to the CROSS leadership team
and the expert skill of Entrusted Word Ministries
for bringing this vision into reality.*

CONTENTS

PROLOGUE

The impetus for this booklet is the CROSS conference of December 2013 in Louisville, KY, USA. We felt compelled to provide an answer to the natural consequents:

> "What happens after CROSS? How can we help young adults move along the path from initial commitment **HERE** to actual arrival **THERE** in missionary service?"

CROSS was launched on the two essential premises:

1. A world and life view grounded in a biblically reformed, theologically high view of God and the Gospel.
2. A strategically focused missiology aimed at reducing the number of unreached people groups (UPGs) in the world, toward fulfilling the Great Commission. The centrality of the glory of Jesus Christ and His Gospel, the sufficiency of Scripture, and sacrificial commitment to reach the heretofore unreached are core themes.

More than 8 out of 10 missionary candidates fail to get to the field. Many intend to go; few make it. Do you want to make it? Do you want to be part of the 15% who actually arrive on the mission field? This book is written for you!

Another conference core theme is the centrality of the local church. The local church, biblically, is both the beginning and the end of missions, and central to God's plan:

> "so that **through the church** the manifold wisdom of God might now be made known to the rulers and authorities in the heavenly places. This was according to the eternal purpose that he has realized in Christ Jesus our Lord ... Now to him who is able to do far more abundantly than all that we ask or think, according to the power at work within us, to him be glory **in the church** and in Christ Jesus throughout all generations, forever and ever. Amen."

> Eph. 3:10-11, 20-21 [emphasis supplied]

The local church's ownership and implementation of the Great Commission supplies a needed component in the process of training, sending, and shepherding qualified missionary workers for long-term ministry among those challenging UPGs. The goal is to proclaim the glory of Christ among UPGs resulting in the planting of indigenous churches **THERE**. Your commitment **HERE** to accomplish that goal goes through your local church.

In these pages, we seek to distill decades of service in church planting, ministry to and among unreached people groups, missions agency leadership, and missions consulting in local churches. Propempo International is committed to coming alongside churches and their missionaries to assist development of biblical, local church-centered missions ministry. We guide paths to missions effectiveness.

We pray that this booklet will be used by Jesus Christ, as Lord of the church, for His glory among the nations. May it be a blessing and practical reference for both the newly committed missionary candidate and his/her local church.

David Meade
Propempo International
David@Propempo.com

GET TALKING!
Share your vision with others

In August 1806, five students at Williams College in Massachusetts informally gathered in a meadow on campus to discuss and pray about the needs of the unreached in Asia, and how they might be personally involved. A storm quickly swept through, forcing the five to take refuge under a haystack. This meeting, later known as the Haystack Prayer Meeting, led to the formation of a student missions mobilization team, and ultimately a mission agency that sent out more than 1,200 missionaries in its first fifty years.

Did God start or strengthen a passion for world missions in you during CROSS, much as He did for those five students? Do you sense that God plans for you to take the Gospel to an unreached corner of the world? We celebrate that with you! Yet it's easy for such an event to become simply a great memory or a binder of notes on a shelf. In this booklet we'd like to help you translate a great experience at CROSS into a great action plan to move you toward the nations, particularly in strong partnership with your home church.

Start your journey by contagiously declaring your passion for the nations to others. It's healthy to be excited about God's work among the nations. It's awe-inspiring to imagine yourself

> Start your journey by contagiously declaring your passion for the nations to others. Give honor and credit to God for His grace and His work that makes it all possible.

helping advance God's Kingdom in a place about which you're concerned. It's normal to want others to feel the same heartbeat for the glory of the Gospel to all nations. Give honor and credit to God for His grace and His work that makes it all possible. Praise Him for including you in His plans.

Key people who need to hear about your plans include:

Your new friends from CROSS. Ask them to pray with you to strengthen your resolve. Ask them to pray for you that God would fulfill your missions goals, according to His will and in His time.

Your friends and family back at home. While they haven't shared the same experience at CROSS that you've had, your excitement can be a contagious part of them beginning to consider their part in God's global mission.

Your campus ministry or young professional fellowship back at home. God may use you as a mobilizer for these people as well.

Your church where you attend during the school year (if a student), **and your home church** (if that's different than the church you attend at school). We'll discuss this more in depth in step 2.

A word of warning:

Do you blog? Are you a regular user of social media (Facebook, Twitter, Google +, Pinterest, Instagram, etc.)? You may be tempted to spill your enthusiasm for unreached people groups in these public arenas. Assume that anything you write publicly will be seen around the world forever. Aspiring missionaries have unwittingly destroyed their chances for entering a creative access country by announcing their future arrival on the Internet. Governments in nations hostile to Christianity are constantly scouring the Internet to prevent missionaries from entering. Don't name people groups in your writing, or use controversial language such as "missionary" or "conversion." Ask your friends to refrain from "sharing" or reposting your writings on these topics.

For additional practical tips, see *Appendix A: Practical Guidelines for Security Concerns.*

Start reading about places and people groups where you might like to serve. Begin enlisting others to stand with you in encouragement and prayer you'll need along the path you are taking.

Simply and humbly share your hopes and dreams. Express your desire to bring God's glory to the unreached. Your testimony will be an encouragement to others. Doing so will reinforce your decision in your own heart and mind. You will begin to grow in faith for the path ahead of you.

A challenging path lies ahead, through all the stages of preparation, qualification, and support raising. Ultimately you'll make very real sacrifices to proclaim the Gospel on your chosen field.

The goal of such communication is to develop a team around you, which you'll need for prayer and support. Unreached people groups are unreached for a reason! The path ahead will require a deep love for God consuming your heart, soul, strength, and mind. Thank God for calling you; plead for His mercy and grace to take you there.

Questions for reflection:

1. Stop and think a moment: Who should be on that list of people you should tell about your new commitment and direction?
2. How will you tell them?
3. How might you follow up to find out how they respond to your news?
4. When you've learned about something as important as missions, it's possible to seem arrogant or judgmental about newfound truth that others haven't learned yet. How can you avoid this kind of posture as you return home?

GET A STRONG FOUNDATION!

Let your church leaders know you want to be sent THERE

The student center at a Christian college featured a wall with posters of local churches with information for securing rides to the churches on Sunday mornings. The wall occasionally featured homemade humorous posters of fictitious churches such as Bedside Baptist Church and The Church of the Holy Comforter (think blanket) that catered to students who found it hard to get out of bed on Sunday morning and connect to a local church!

If you're a student or recent graduate, you're probably familiar with the temptation to skip church, perpetually visit many churches, or depend more on a campus parachurch ministry (RUF, Campus Outreach, IVCF, Navigators, CRU, etc.) for discipleship and community. Yet the Bible places the local church at the heart of the missionary sending process. You can read some of the biblical reasons why the local church is central in *Step 3: Get Experience!*

Before leaving for the field you should demonstrate a healthy connection with and approval of the local church that's willing to send you. Your church and missions agency will require it. Your likelihood of surviving and thriving on the field directly

> **Having a strong local sending church as the core of your support team is essential to your long-term effectiveness.**

correlates to a healthy church that proactively helped you prepare for and get to the field. So, your very next step on the path from **HERE** to **THERE** is to bring your local church into the picture.

Many young missionary candidates, with surging eagerness to hurry to the field, short circuit or neglect involving their home (sending) church early in the process. If you're away from your home church during college years, this might be difficult. However, having a strong local sending church as the core of your support team is essential to your long-term effectiveness.

Measuring the health of your relationship with your current home [sending] church

How would you answer the following questions?

- Are you an active member in a local church at all? (You'll need to find a strong local church. More on that later.)
- Is missions an evident passion and purpose of your home church? Growing a missions passion may need some help from you or outside resources.
- What kind of relationship do you have with your church leadership?
- Have you had an active role in ministry in or through your church?
- Has your church tracked your spiritual health and maturity while you've been away at college/university? To whom are you spiritually accountable in your church? (e.g. a small group leader, staff pastor, an older mentor, or a ministry group leader?) Ask your home church who might serve as such a key contact for you while you finish college.
- How long has your church known of your interest in missions?

If you or your family have not been active members of a good Bible teaching, missions-minded local church, this must become one of your highest priorities after leaving CROSS.

How do you find a local church capable of sending you well?

Here are some guidelines.

1. **Are you in agreement with the church's doctrinal stance?** If you're in agreement with the theology that you've heard at the CROSS conference, then you'll want to carefully read the doctrinal statement or "statement of faith" of your prospective sending church. Pray for understanding; get help from a mature believer in discerning the strength and accuracy of the doctrinal statement. Here are a few key elements you should look for clear statements on:

   - The sovereignty and deity of God in Three Persons.
   - The inspiration, inerrancy and sufficiency of the Scripture as the final authority.
   - The perfect life, substitutionary death and resurrection of the Lord Jesus Christ in the place of sinners.
   - The depravity and utter inability of man to merit or cause his own salvation apart from the intervention of God's grace and mercy in salvation through repentance and faith in Christ alone.

- The glory of God as the ultimate purpose of all that God does.

2. **How important is missions to this church?** If possible, become a part of a church that already loves missions and has a reputation as a missionary sending church. How "visible" is missions in its sermons, literature, lobby and worship center? Ask questions. Find out how they "do missions." Who leads missions? (a staff member? a missions team?) Ask for a copy of any missions policy or strategy. Find out whom the church supports, and where they serve. Does the church have a written plan for developing and training "homegrown" missionaries?

Characteristics of a Strong Missions-Minded Church

The following descriptions indicate a church that is growing into a model that reflects God's heart for the nations:

- The church possesses a scriptural understanding of:
  - God's purpose in this world: that He be glorified and worshipped throughout the earth among all people groups.
  - The role of the local church in fulfilling God's purpose.
- The pastor and church leaders provide mission vision in the church, working with all ministry staff and ministries to inculcate a passion for global evangelization.
- Church members realize their essential roles in the Great Commission and exercise World Christian priorities in fulfilling His global purpose.
- Global missions has been integrated into the culture of the church in such a way that it has become a part of the DNA identity of the church.

- The church's missions strategy includes a balanced strategy for both local and global aspects of its missions outreach.
- The church has a Missions Committee, Board, or Team to facilitate the mobilization and involvement of the whole congregation in the church's missions strategy and outreach.
- The church systematically prays for and holistically supports its supported ministries and missionaries.
- Short-term missions are vibrant parts both of discipling its members as World Christians, and making win-win-win contributions to field ministries, missionaries, and their target population.
- The church has a vision to identify, train, and send missionary candidates from the congregation, in alignment with the church's chosen strategy/ies.
- The church has developed and implemented a written missions policy, which includes strategy for involvement, care for missionaries, and other guidelines.
- The church invests a significant amount of its funds in world missions.
- The church hosts a regular world missions event, celebrating what God is doing in and through the church globally.
- Missions is frequently communicated through all the ministries of the church (worship, prayer, preaching, teaching, education, training, discipleship, small groups, youth, Sunday School, men's and ladies groups, etc.) throughout the year.

> With some patience and passion, you can be instrumental in helping your church become your most important long-term asset in reaching "your" unreached people group.

Get good counsel from mature Christian friends about your choice of a local church. This is an important decision to be made for sound biblical reasons rather than personal preferences or consumer-oriented reasons. Great churches feature sound teaching, a good shepherding atmosphere, gracious and loving fellowship, and a commitment to know, love and proclaim the Gospel. Check out Mark Dever's *Nine Marks of a Healthy Church* (Crossway, 2004).

Here are some suggested standards that would indicate a good **sending** church:

1. The sending church has developed clear expectations and a process or path for becoming a missionary sent from the church.
2. The sending church understands and affirms the obligation of the church to guide and manage the development of their missionary in issues such as character, ministry competency (including language and cultural acquisition and adjustment), doctrinal integrity, and direction/allocation on the field.
3. In addition to the elders' general oversight, the sending church provides a mentor and/or "Barnabas Team" advocate person or team.
4. The sending church confirms a mutually acceptable comprehensive support schedule and helps the missionary raise those funds through accountability, advocacy and active assistance.
5. The sending church commits to appropriate communication and shepherding on the field.
6. The sending church intelligently interacts with ministry decisions and strategy on the field.

7. The sending church proactively and annually evaluates the health, ministry and working relationships of the field missionary (and family, if applicable).

No church is perfect, and it may be tempting to get to the field quicker by taking shortcuts around a substantial sending church relationship. As the African proverb says, "If you want to travel fast, travel alone; if you want to travel far, travel together." This is applicable to a sending church relationship. Your impact on the field will be deeper and longer with a great sending church behind you. It may even mean helping your church become the sending church it needs to be. It's worth the hard work. With some patience and passion, you can be instrumental in helping your church become your most important long-term asset in reaching "your" unreached people group.

We'll leave you with quotes from two wise missions leaders on the importance of mobilization:

> "Suppose I had a thousand college seniors in front of me who asked me where they ought to go to make a maximum contribution to Christ's global cause. What would I tell them? I would tell them to mobilize [i.e. – be instrumental in sending out others]. All of them."
>
> —Dr. Ralph Winter
> founder of the US Center For World Mission

> "Someone must sound the rallying call. Those who desire to see others trained, prepared and released to ministry are known as mobilizers. Mobilizers stir other Christians to active concern for reaching the world. Mobilizers are essential. To understand the role of mobilizers, think of World War II as a parallel. Only 10% of the American

population went to the war. Of those, only 1% were actually on the firing lines. However, for them to be successful in their mission, the entire country had to be mobilized!"

—Phil Parshall
missionary to the Muslim world

Questions for reflection:

1. What should you do right now to get better connected to a good sending church?

2. Who do you know that might be an advocate for your missionary candidacy with your church?

3. What steps can you take soon that would cultivate prayer from your church for your missions path from **HERE** to **THERE**?

Resources:

These books will give you a sound overview of what makes a healthy, biblical church, why the church is central to missions ministry, and what it means to be an active church member.

Mark Dever, *Nine Marks of a Healthy Church* (Crossway, 2004)

Patrick Johnstone, *The Church is Bigger Than You Think* (Christian Focus, 2000)

Joshua Harris, *Why Church Matters* (Multnomah, 2011)

Thabiti Anyabwile, *What is a Healthy Church Member?* (Crossway, 2008)

David Platt, *Radical Together* (Multnomah, 2011)

GET EXPERIENCE!

Sharpen your skills for the field through practical experience in ministry.

In the remake of *The Karate Kid*, Dre Parker (played by Jaden Smith) finds himself in China with no friends in a strange land. He becomes the bullying object of a group of teen karate students. Dre discovers that the maintenance man, Mr. Han (played by Jackie Chan), is secretly a Kung Fu master, and persuades Mr. Han to train him. The early days of training prove exasperating, as Mr. Han's instruction calls for seemingly irrelevant repetition of activities unrelated to karate.

Dre allows himself to believe that Mr. Han isn't really capable of training him in martial arts, and complains. Mr. Han patiently pushes Dre to see that the very repetitive motions required of him are the basic moves he needs to defend himself with karate. Suddenly the training makes sense. The menial repetitive motions have equipped him for his journey toward becoming a gifted young karate champion.

Much as Dre needed training, arguably the most essential step toward the mission field is developing the ministry skills in and through a local church setting that you'll need on the field. The apostle Paul, the greatest missionary in church history, is a highly appropriate example of this truth.

1. **The church at Antioch observed Paul doing significant ministry in the church at Antioch for several years** before he was released to the mission field (Acts 11.25-26). In fact, Paul was "in training" for as much as twelve years between

the time of his conversion and "call" to missions and his actual departure for missionary work.

2. **Paul did not simply volunteer to go to the field**. The elders set him apart through the direction of the Holy Spirit (Acts 13:1-3). While this incident is not typical, and while it is not wrong to volunteer for the mission field, confirmation of "the call" does not happen in a vacuum. Michael Griffiths writes, "The most that an individual can do is express his willingness. Others must determine his worthiness. The individual may be free to go, but only his church knows if he is really fitted to go." (in *Get Your Church Involved in Missions!*)

Confirmation of the missionary call happens in a local church setting. If friends and leaders in your local church context don't see missionary qualities in you first-hand, then you may not be ready to go.

The local church attests to the veracity of God's calling as it confirms your mix of gifts, skills, training and inclination. The Bible does not authorize missionary candidates to "lay hands on" themselves.

Let this sink in! It is important for you to understand and make it practical in your spiritual values and priorities:

The local church is central to God's plan for ministry and missions to all nations!

Here is a simple overview of biblical principles showing the centrality of the local church in understanding its priority for the task of missions.

Briefly:

1. Those who received the Great Commission directly–the Apostles, their contemporaries, and their helpers–fulfilled the mandate by planting and organizing indigenous churches (see all the book of Acts!). They understood that the fruit of obedience to the Great Commission resulted in the establishment of new local churches everywhere.

2. The Great Commission, as expressed in Matthew 28:16-20, cannot be fulfilled apart from a mutually committed group of believers meeting together for worship, teaching, and edification, under biblically recognized church leadership, and observing the ordinances given by Christ. i.e. – **The natural product of completely fulfilling the Great Commission is local churches.**

3. The vast majority of New Testament epistles were addressed to local churches or leaders of local churches. This presumes the local church to be the nexus of the practice of Christian life and maturity.

4. Jesus' promise to build His church (Matthew 16:18) and biblical teaching regarding church discipline (see Matthew 18:15-20, and all of 1 Corinthians) is set in the context of the local church.

5. Jesus' messages to "the seven churches of Asia" (Rev. 2-3) speak to the significance and centrality of local churches in the perspective of Christ, some 60 years after the giving of the Great Commission.

6. The 40+ "one another" commands of the New Testament all refer to the dynamic relationships of Christians within a local church context.

7. The local church in Antioch is the scriptural setting through which the Holy Spirit worked to set apart the first New Testament missionaries. Clearly, in the outlook of Paul and Barnabas, the local church is intended as the initiator, the means, and the ends of Gospel missions ministry.

8. Paul appeals to the local church of Rome to partner with him in his pioneering aspirations for the last unreached area of the Mediterranean basin, the Iberian Peninsula, "Spain" (Romans 15:18-29). The reason behind Paul's letter to the Philippians is to thank them for their ongoing financial support and encouragement. His relationship to that local church as a partner in his missionary ministry was a source of great joy and enablement. The relationship and accountability to his first "sending" church at Antioch is a model for all missionaries.

9 With Apostolic authority from Christ, Paul charges his colleagues, Timothy and Titus, to organize local churches and appoint spiritually qualified leaders in them. His goal, apparently, was to see indigenous local churches as the fruit of his and their work.

10. John appeals to a church leader, Gaius, to continue his church's good work of lavishly loving and providing for the needs of Gospel workers. Indeed, this responsibility is described as the privilege and duty of the local church body, as partners in the truth with missionaries. (3 John 5-8)

11. The local church validates and approves workers set apart for ministry. (Acts 13:1-3; 14:26-28; 16:1-3; 1 Timothy 3:1-7; 5:22; Titus 1:5-9)

Your best laboratory for developing ministry skills and experience is in and through your local church. Why is this ministry so foundational?

- **Changing geography won't make you a missionary.** A plane trip places you in an even more difficult ministry setting. You won't magically begin doing on foreign soil what you haven't already been doing at home.

- **Local church ministry simulates many situations you'll encounter on the field**, where things rarely go as planned. Personalities clash. You don't get your way. You have to follow a leader, policy or direction you may not value. People you're supposed to be leading might not value you or your leadership. And you may be expected to do things that you think are lowly and demeaning.

- **Ministry in and through the local church is a sanctifying instrument of God** to make you more like Christ. Use It to develop field essential perspectives, such as "What can I learn? What does this expose in my heart that needs God's grace? How can I grow from this?" If this is your response to ministry experience, then you'll be on track for missionary qualification. If, on the other hand, you're thinking, "I hate this! There is no redeeming value in what I'm doing here!, Why can't my leaders just recognize my superlative quality and send me out right away?", then you'll be on track for disqualification.

How much time does this step take? Take a deep breath: it takes longer than you might think. But after you've done it, it will seem that it went by faster than you expected. Don't worry! A lot of the "to do" items are overlapping and simultaneous, not separate and sequential. You're preparing for a lifetime of strategic ministry. A few months or years **HERE** enabling and equipping you to survive and thrive **THERE** will be worth every moment. None of it is wasted time in God's good providence. Everything in your life is a prologue for what God has yet for you to do. The preparation is as much your calling and ministry in God's will as the "actual" work on the field.

> Everything in your life is a prologue for what God has yet for you to do. The preparation is as much your calling and ministry in God's will as the "actual" work on the field.

Even more important than ministry skills is a missionary's character. Missionaries should expect to meet the same stringent biblical requirements of pastor-elders in their home congregation (cf. Acts 16:2; 1 Timothy 3; Titus 1).

What might your home church expect in preparing for the mission field?

Here are some potential pre-field requirements gleaned from the missionary preparation programs of several leading churches:

1. Required reading (typically 50-100 pages of focused reading per week)
2. Mentoring by a trusted, mature believer
3. Active ministry
4. A spectrum of missions-related skill building (cross-cultural exposure, novice language learning, evangelism, discipling/training, small group leadership, etc.)
5. Submitting progress reports to, and prayer with, the Missions Pastor or Missions Team
6. Leadership training classes and experiences

7. Research or reflection papers or presentations
8. Leading and organizing a short term missions team or project
9. Starting a prayer group for a country, world region or an unreached people group
10. Researching potential mission agency partners
11. Addressing issues that surface through biblical counseling
12. Biblical and theological training
13. Teaching and/or discipleship experience
14. Completing a physical check up
15. Business training, experience, and certifications, especially if you are planning on working in business on the field
16. Church planting training/internship
17. Training in interpersonal relationships and team-building
18. Training in security and crisis issues
19. Training in technology and computer applications

What if your church doesn't have a systematic plan for developing future missionaries?

How can you help your church grow in missionary preparation?

- **Pray.** Pray with church leaders about their role and responsibility in sending you out. Ask prayer partners to pray with you about this issue. As possible and appropriate, get out prayer information to the church regarding your church's process of sending you. God hears and answers prayer. He asks us to pray. So pray expecting Him to answer.

- **Serve as a facilitator and catalyst.** View your role as one of practical encourager rather than critic. Lay before God any frustration with your church. What you're doing for your church and its future is priceless.

- **Serve as a resource.** A variety of fine resources are available to help a church grow in this process. Bring your church's leaders into contact with key books, websites and individuals who can help your church move forward as a sender. Suggest resources sparingly; avoid overwhelming your leaders with ideas. And do it all with a spirit of humility.

- **Serve as a networker.** Reach out to mature, sympathetic and respected fellow church members to assist in the process. Proactively set up appointments for formal and/or informal discussions to work on the details of developing as a sending church. Meet leaders at their convenience. For example, have an early coffee or breakfast meeting with a lay leader before his work hours. Be obvious in your goals without being obnoxious.

If your church is a larger church, keep in mind:

- It will take more time and energy to affect a change in strategy or direction.
- You will need to convince more leaders.
- The church can offer more resources for sending missionaries.

If your church is a smaller or medium-sized church, keep in mind:

- It will likely take less effort to help the church recognize and embrace its biblical responsibilities in missionary sending.

- Relationships with leadership and among leadership are that much closer. Communication lines are simpler and more direct. You will have more access to and relationship with its pastors and leaders.

If your church doesn't currently systematically prepare missionaries, how can you begin to prepare on your own?

Here's a list of great learning activities.

- It's critical for your missions motivation to flow out of the biblical concept of the glory of God and His global purpose to see Jesus Christ glorified in all nations. There is perhaps no better treatment of this topic than *Let the Nations Be Glad* by John Piper.

- Enroll in survey or overview classes in Bible and systematic theology. Lots of resources are now available online. See some example resources below.

- Cultivate a high view of Scripture: a commitment to know it, obey it, apply it, teach it, proclaim it.

- Test your interests, gifts and skills in a variety of ministry settings such as ministry to children and youth, evangelism, and small group leadership.

- Prayerfully identify a mentor or prayer partner who will be ruthlessly honest with you in evaluating your spiritual maturity, relationships, and personality.

- Seek out opportunities for local cross-cultural ministry similar to the place or culture you'd like to serve.

- Grow in initiative. Practice looking for a service or ministry need and doing it without being asked. A church planter must be a person of initiative and proactivity. Learn to see needs and priorities and to act on them now.

- Share the Gospel consistently. Part of the joy of missionary life is weaving the proclamation of the Gospel into every relationship and many conversations.

- Develop a vibrant and consistent personal devotional life. On the field you will be largely dependent on your own discipline for spiritual feeding and vitality. You won't have the same resources as you do back home. Learn how to worship and grow and savor and delight in God and His Word without being dependent on people or resources only available here.

- While we will all be imperfect and broken people until heaven, the Bible's standards for those who would start and lead churches, and influence people for Christ, are high. The goal in your character is to be "above reproach" (1 Timothy 3). Use this time of preparation on the path to the field to deal aggressively with besetting sins, personality quirks and offensive hindrances that will both hurt intimacy with God and also erode your effectiveness on the field. So, if there are habits that need to be broken or reformed, seek help to do it now. God not only calls you to holiness, He also supplies abundant grace for your journey. The path to genuine, heart-driven holiness is described in Phil. 2:12-13: "work out your own salvation with fear and trembling, for it is God who works in you, both to will and to work for his good pleasure." Simply trying harder does not work. You are partners with God in sanctification. A lifestyle of repentance orients you to see, confess, mourn and eventually hate our sin. Also, you learn to remove obstacles to spiritual progress in your life. For example, if you can't get up in the morning to read the Bible because you stay up late watching TV, then you figure out that you can't keep doing that and expect to grow. If that is the case, you value Christ over TV and stop watching TV at night or disconnect the cable. God uses these cumulative offerings to effect the character change that only He can. His mercy and grace can transform your heart as you become a useful vessel in His service. The humility and integrity you will build in the process are irreplaceable foundation stones for your character as you prepare to go.

Questions for reflection:

1. Is the centrality of the local church for missionary preparation a new or surprising concept for you? Is this concept freeing or frustrating to you? Why?

2. Have you had any past experiences with local churches that now erode your confidence in working with your church on the way to the field? What will be necessary to overcome this lack of trust as you now move toward the field?

3. How much of a temptation is it for you to hurry to the field? Why? How can you balance an appropriate urgency with a willingness to be prepared as necessary?

Resources

Brian Croft, *Test, Train, Affirm, and Send Into Ministry* (Day One Publications, 2010). Croft's book is aimed at preparing U.S.-based ministry staff; but the application to preparing missionaries is perfect. You and your church leaders should definitely get and implement this book.

The **www.Prompempo.com** website offers many links and recommendations to many PDFs, books, and external resources, including an array of church-based missionary candidate training and mentoring models.

There are lots of online training resources out there. Some are better than others. Some you should just avoid because of defective doctrine. Get some advice from trusted leaders. Here are a few places to begin your search for biblical training online:

> *www.covenantseminary.edu/resources*
> *www.sbts.edu/online*
> *www.ligonier.org/learn/series*
> *http://rts.edu/site/Global/About*

GET CONNECTED!
Select a mission agency primed
to partner with you and your church

While a missionary couple dined in a North African restaurant one night, the wife suffered a medical emergency and collapsed unconscious on the floor. Regardless of how well meaning their home church in Connecticut was, this couple needed a mission agency's immediate expertise on the ground to evacuate her by plane to England for emergency brain surgery.

A team in North Africa, sent without the help of a mission agency, was poised to sign a major business deal that would have established an important presence in that nation. When the North African business partner realized at the table that the team could not speak French, the official language of business, the deal collapsed. The team had to leave for France for six months of language training. A mission agency with experience in the region could have helped avert this serious misstep.

These are but two examples of why your choice of a mission agency partner is critical. That's why your church's first time to hear of your agency choice should never be at the point of requesting your pastor to sign an agency's pastoral reference form. This is a decision best made jointly with your sending church.

Hopefully by now you are convinced of a strong, local church-centered ministry philosophy. Yet your church's heart to be deeply involved in your ministry does not negate the usefulness of having a partnership relationship with a reputable sending agency. You'll need prayerful discernment as you and your church leaders sift

through the information and promotional materials. Asking the right questions will save you a lot of headache and surprises down the road.

Why do you need a mission agency?

For a variety of theological and practical reasons some churches and missionaries question the need for a mission agency. After all, the churches in Acts directly sent missionaries. And at first glance it seems much less expensive to bypass the mission agency.

Local churches tend to overestimate their abilities and underestimate the complexities of functioning as their own mission agency. What the local church doesn't pay in fees to the mission agency, costs a tremendous amount of time and effort managing complex details and decisions at a far distance. Managing and supporting a missionary thousands of miles away in a radically different cultural context is completely different than managing staff at the church.

A well-selected mission agency lends its specialized expertise, adding benefits and help to the local church in managing some complex issues, including:

- Retirement plans
- Group health insurance
- Field supervision and accountability
- Language study
- Financial management involving foreign currency
- Compliance with tax codes and requirements
- Experienced strategy and personnel management
- Visa and immigration legalities
- Corporate identity and team issues in the target country

> Local churches tend to overestimate their abilities and underestimate the complexities of functioning as their own mission agency.

Should you serve with your denomination's mission agency?

The answer is: very possibly! If your church is part of a denomination, you and your church leaders might automatically assume that you should serve with your denomination's mission agency. It could well be the best fit. However, it would probably be a mistake to make that assumption without also asking the right questions to help confirm your decision.

What are the questions you should be asking about potential mission agency partners? Here are some important places to start.

1. **What's the agency's doctrinal statement?** This area is of paramount importance. It drives every agency's field ministry and leadership decisions. You'll want substantial

agreement in doctrine rather than general agreement over a broad "evangelical" statement of faith. How does its doctrinal statement compare with your church's doctrinal statement in the following areas?

- God's sovereignty
- The sufficiency of Scripture
- A God-centered view of salvation
- Agreement with the five *solas* of the historical Reformation
- Strength in the primary matters of the Gospel (such as the deity of the Triune God and the exclusivity of the Gospel)
- Appropriate freedom in secondary matters, matters of Christian conscience, and disciplinary issues

2. **How does the agency operate financially?** Consider at least three key areas.

- **How are you expected to raise financial support?** Most typical is an individualized system, where the agency releases to you only funds given for you. In a pooling system, teams, regions or even the entire agency divide(s) up the pool of funds received. Some denominations, particularly the Christian and Missionary Alliance and Southern Baptists, pay missionaries from denominational funds, with missionaries needing to raise no personalized support.

- **What is the agency's monthly administrative fee?** It costs money for a mission agency to provide services for you while you're on the field. The agency receives and transmits your incoming support, finds good health insurance for you, and provides you with a team on the field, to name a few functions. Sometimes this fee also helps pay for services originating on the field. At least a portion of this cost is passed on to missionaries in the form of administrative fees that are part of your support package. Depending on the amount and quality of services provided, you will be assessed a share of the administrative costs, usually a percentage between 3%-25% of your monthly support package. In some rare cases the costs could be up to 40% of income of the mission. This percentage is usually between 9-15%.

- **Does the agency operate with financial integrity?** Does the agency conduct regular audits according to standard accounting principles? (Membership in an organization such as Mission Nexus or the Evangelical Council for Financial Accountability requires such standards.) What is its policy and track record regarding internal borrowing? Private inurement? Conflict of interest? Corporate debt? Who are its board members, and on what basis were they selected? How is the support level for the field determined? How well or poorly are the needs of its workers accommodated by their support level?

3. **Is the agency experienced in your ministry or region?** You'll want to choose a mission that has specific experience and skill in the particular type of ministry or location to which you are going. If you are beginning ministry to a previously unengaged people group, the agency should have experience in entering similar settings.

4. **How is the agency organized to lead the work on the field?** At issue here is how much autonomy you and your team will be given to carry out the ministry. More hierarchically organized agencies make ministry decisions in the home office and hand down directives to the field. Decentralized agencies give virtually complete freedom to the team on the field. In the middle are agencies that give substantial

freedom to teams, subject to oversight by one or more layers of field leadership (leaders over teams, countries and regions). Are you and your church comfortable with the agency's leadership structures?

5. **How willing is the agency to partner with your church?** The answer to this question can be a deal breaker with your church. If your church wants to authentically partner with you and your ministry, the prospective mission agency partner must allow for an enlarged role for your sending church. See some of the sample terms in *Appendix B: A Sample Sending Church - Mission Agency Partnership Agreement (simplified)*.

6. **What is the agency's missiological framework and strategy?** Put more simply, what methodologies and principles direct the agency's ministry decisions and practices, particularly in church planting? Does the agency tend toward more traditional or trendy approaches? Problems are associated with both ends of this spectrum. Some traditional approaches may no longer be effective. Trendy practices may spring from theologically questionable pragmatism with untested long-term results.

7. **How does the agency relate to indigenous Christians on the field?** Some agencies have pre-established relationships with an indigenous church body in your target area which could impact your ministry. Other agencies avoid restrictive ministry relationships with indigenous Christians in order to plant churches "from scratch." Still other agencies may insist that you work under the direction and control of local Christian leadership.

8. **What quality of member care does the agency provide?** What are the agency's resources and plan for supervising,

shepherding and nurturing you while on the field? To what extent does the agency welcome your church's visiting and shepherding you on the field? What are the responsibilities and obligations of mission members during home assignments? What are the policies regarding time away from field ministry for vacation, training, short home visits and further education?

9. **What does the agency's "Member Handbook" tell you?**
An agency should be glad to let you read its manual of organizational policies. It's a helpful glance inside the organization that will inform you on issues such as:

- Rules and regulations for behavior
- Organizational structure
- Expectations for accountability and reporting
- Support requirements and expectations
- Administrative costs

While the handbook probably won't be a major factor in deciding on an agency, its description of the agency's organizational culture may tip the balance in favor of one over another.

10. **How does the agency address current issues and trends?**
Read through the agency's statements of policies or

principles regarding current trends in mission strategies, such as the "Insider Movement" (a contextualization issue).

What should you expect in the application process?

Once you've chosen your sending agency, you'll apply to become a member. This process will include:

- **References:** You'll be asked to provide character references from your church, school, workplace and friends. The agency will likely ask your references for other references.

- **Bible and doctrine assessment:** You'll usually take standardized tests to determine your basic Bible knowledge and theological understanding. The best doctrinal exams will frame questions in a field context, such as, "Over coffee, a Muslim friend asks you to explain the Trinity..." Ideally, the mission will provide both a score and feedback to you regarding your results on the tests.

- **Psychological testing:** Though the effectiveness of secular normed standardized psychological testing is questionable, many agencies use this means to discern aberrant behavior or weaknesses that could become a liability or disqualification for field service. We encourage a more biblical approach of relationship and discipleship tailored to building leadership character (e.g. 1 Tim. 3, "above reproach") of ministry leaders. If you and your church leaders work with you through your answers to direct, probing questions, that process will be worth more. See *Appendix C: 21 Questions for Missionary Candidates.*

After reviewing your application, the mission agency may extend an invitation for you to attend its one or two week Candidate Orientation School (or equivalent) at its headquarters and at your own cost. The agency is relying heavily on your references and test results, along with orientation, to make a decision on offering you membership. Your local church should know you far better than what the agency can know about you through a relatively limited process. This is why your church's recommendation is arguably the most important element of your application.

Candidate Orientation usually includes the following elements:

- An introduction to the agency's history and vision
- A virtual tour of the agency's fields of service and types of ministries
- An intensive series of interviews and evaluations
- Pointed questions about your testimony, personal life and ministry experience
- Instruction about expectations, requirements, and public image as a member of the mission
- Instruction about fund-raising and accountability

If you have been diligent in preparing, you will probably receive a letter of acceptance with contingencies. The contingencies will address specific needs for personal growth, development, and/or skill building and requirements for your prospective specific field and ministry.

You'll be expected to sign a formal acceptance paper, granting you all the terms, rights and responsibilities of membership. Depending on its pre-field requirements, personalized preparation and contingencies, you then officially become a missionary member of that organization.

While you may be a fully accepted member of your mission agency, you may still need to fulfill certain requirements for your church before it releases you to raise funds and book tickets for the field.

Though not common, it's ideal for your sending church and sending agency to draft a written partnership agreement or memo of understanding to secure their ongoing role in your ministry direction, shepherding, and evaluation. See: *Appendix B: A Sample Sending Church - Mission Agency Partnership Agreement (simplified)*

Now you begin the path of focused preparation for field ministry.

Questions for reflection:

1. What's most important to you about the mission agency you would join? Why?

2. Does your sending church have strong relationships with any mission agencies, and if so, which ones? Are any of these possibilities?

3. Have you participated in any agency's short-term trips? What did you like about those agencies? What did you dislike?

Resources

Corbett and Fikkert, *When Helping Hurts.* This is in the top five books we would require of every missionary candidate. It helps the reader grasp a realistic and effective approach to dealing with extreme poverty and human needs.

David Horne, *When Missions Shapes the Mission of the Church.* Horne tells it like it is from the perspective of a missions-minded 30-year pastoral ministry in a significant SBC church in Raleigh NC. If you are from a Southern Baptist background, it's an eye-opening read, full of great missions quotes.

Here are a couple of practical web pages for your agency search process:

James Rutz, *How Do I Choose a Mission Agency?*
http://cart2pioneers.org/frd/MI_MissionAgencies.pdf

World Venture, *How To Choose A Mission Agency*
http://www.worldventure.com/document.doc?id=65

GET FOCUSED!

Learn all you can about cross-cultural church planting

Sylvia went to the Candidate Orientation of a major mission agency to become a church planter. She came with full recommendation by her church regarding her preparedness to enter such a ministry. In her interview with a committee, she was asked how she discipled people, and whom she was currently discipling. Her refreshingly honest yet deeply disturbing answer was, "I've never been discipled, so I don't know how to disciple people."

Such an answer is more common than might be imagined. Many missionaries come to mission agencies for acceptance while having very little experience in the basics of evangelism and discipleship. Few have ever worshipped in truly disciple-making churches. Yet these missionaries plan to plant churches in the most difficult places around the world. Many missionaries aiming at church planting among unreached people groups have little first-hand knowledge and experience in a healthy church.

It's true that an overseas church will and should look quite different than "the one back home." A church's culture, language, dress, musical expression and liturgy will look quite different in a large wealthy suburb of Minneapolis than in a slum of Cairo. Take time to study the Bible and make decisions about what minimal elements should be present in a biblically functioning local church. Here's a suggested starting list:

- a mutually committed body of local believers
- worshiping regularly together

- around the teaching of the Word of God and prayer
- observing the ordinances of baptism and communion
- under the leadership of biblically qualified shepherds
- while being active witnesses of the Gospel

Likewise, a biblical definition of a local church eliminates some elements as not biblically essential for a local church, particularly in an unreached people group context:

- paid pastors and staff
- programs
- Sunday School
- choir
- youth group
- printed curriculum
- buildings
- offering plates
- a particular style of music
- electronic musical instruments
- a particular size of congregation/audience
- corporate worship on Sunday morning
- mid-week prayer service
- sound amplification
- LCD projectors

How can you get church planting training before going overseas?

Arguably the best pre-field experience you'll receive is ministry in and through the context of a healthy, biblically led, disciple-making local church. It is difficult to imagine entering a difficult, resistant part of the world to plant churches without such experience. If your church is starting a new campus or planting a daughter church, consider helping as part of the start up team for that new church.

Even if your church is not directly involved in church planting, you can find a nearby like-minded church plant in which you can observe, intern, or assist. Check out your local Gospel Coalition regional fellowship. Seek contacts through your church leaders or other trusted church leaders. At the very least, get involved in, and ideally lead, a disciple-making small group or missional community in your church.

Pre-field cross-cultural church planting experience can be an invaluable asset to field effectiveness. That experience will clarify and temper your expectations for ministry. One of the most common factors in missionaries leaving the field is unrealistic expectations. Even a little experience **HERE** can inject realism into your expectations **THERE**.

> Arguably the best pre-field experience you'll receive is ministry in and through the context of a healthy, biblically led, disciple-making local church.

Field workers need to understand their target culture and the delicate interpersonal challenges of discipling new believers and developing biblically qualified church leaders. Ideally you're looking for a church planting experience in a linguistic and cultural setting similar to your future place of service. Most major cities in the US allow easy access to immigrants from many unreached people groups. US Census demographic data can help identify your nearest opportunity. Ask around to discover any ethnic churches in your area that might have connections or some relationship with your target group **THERE**.

You may need to develop courage and initiative to visit an international market and find people from or from near your target unreached people group. If you do, strive to learn all you can by asking questions. Be persistent without becoming threatening. Whatever relationships, language and cultural connections you can make here will give you a running start when you land on the field.

Finally, some of your best mentors can come in the form of books. Many current resources on church planting and cross-cultural church planting methodologies are available in seminary libraries, Christian bookstores, and online. The best ones are rooted in simple biblical basics.

A missiologically sound cross-cultural church planting process compels the missionary to:

1. Learn the language and culture of the recipients or target group as the first priority.
2. Model the development of a plurality of local leaders from the earliest stages of spiritual growth.
3. Focus on the Bible as the source of authoritative guidance for the new believers and the newly forming church.

4. Use only locally acceptable and reproducible methods and means of ministry.

The church planting process universally involves a continuous cycle of:

- Evangelism
- Discipleship
- Leadership development
- Smaller gatherings for teaching and worship
- Aggregation of several smaller gatherings
- Recognition of local leaders and teachers
- Recognition and affirmation of a local church body
- Extending the cycle to plant other churches

Once the cycle begins, each earlier stage continues as new steps begin.

What if I'm not going to plant churches?

An increasing number of missionaries' and agencies' ministries primarily address issues of social justice and relief and development. These ministries may include evangelism, but they lack a focus of intentional church planting. While caring for orphans, digging wells for clean water, and stopping sex trafficking are good and biblical ministries, we would argue that the core mandate of the Great Commission is disciple making. And where authentic disciples emerge, churches start.

If your goal is not disciple-making that ultimately leads to the founding of healthy churches, we'd encourage you to study the Bible carefully. Examine Jesus' commands, Paul's missionary strategies, and the early church's legacy of church multiplication. You can engage in social justice and relief/development ministries that are either ends to themselves, or that are attached to a team's larger church planting goals. We would encourage the latter. To see a rationale for this, go to *Appendix D: Why "church planting" is THE priority ministry in missions*.

Gaining insight from personal church planting involvement and learning vicariously from experienced missionaries are invaluable. Ask lots of questions. Be prepared to have your assumptions challenged. Church planting is not an exact science. When church planting among the least reached peoples of the world, you are treading in territory that the enemy will not release without a fight. The challenges of cross-cultural church planting, perceived correctly, will drive you to a desperate dependence upon a sovereign God to move and to build His Church.

Questions for reflection:

1. How would you define "church"? What are the absolute biblical essentials? What are the non-essentials?

2. How would your definition of "church" impact your perspective on what the church might look like **THERE**, in your mission field?

3. Set up a time to discuss church planting philosophy with an experienced pastor or missionary over coffee or pizza.

4. What assumptions have you had previously about "church" that you now see as non-essential?

Resources:

Websites such as *www.islamicfinder.org* allow you to enter a zip code and find local mosques and Muslim-owned businesses.

Here are some classic materials on the purpose of the church and practical missiology on church planting. You won't have time to study all of them; but you could learn a lot by reading and interacting with one or two; then see where those lead you for further study.

DeYoung and Gilbert, *What is the Mission of the Church?* (Crossway, 2011)

David Hesselgrave, *Planting Churches Cross-Culturally* (Baker, 2000)

J.D. Payne, *Discovering Church Planting* (Paternoster, 2009)

Sherwood Lingenfelter, *Ministering Cross-Culturally* (Baker, 2003)

Patterson and Scoggins, *Church Multiplication Guide* (William Carey Library, 2002)

GET APPROVED!
Fulfill your mission agency's pre-field requirements

One western US local church sent a team to a Muslim nation without the help of an agency and its pre-field training requirements. The team of three literally wandered the country on tourist visas seeking a way to begin ministry. Giving away used clothes was their first strategy, and when this didn't produce many results, they decided to gain English teaching credentials online. They were unsure how to secure ESL jobs, and after months operating with a language barrier, they finally decided that they might need to learn the nation's language. They left the country and began language learning.

Meanwhile, still with good motives, this same church sent a short-term team in to the same country to aggressively distribute gospel tracts. For the sake of plausible deniability, the short termers deliberately did not let any in-country missionaries know of their coming. They began entering small mountain villages and giving out tracts. When local authorities were tipped off to the activity, the team fled into the mountain wilderness to camp for a few days while things settled down. Without optimal camping gear in the cold nights, the team got sick, had to discontinue its work, and left the country after two weeks and with very little helpful ministry accomplished.

Mission agencies offer experience that can help local churches send missionaries well. The training they require helps missionaries and their churches avoid wasting precious time and resources as is evident in the stories above.

Rare is the future missionary who leaves a mission agency's orientation with no required preparation before departure. Let's examine what agencies typically require before giving you the green light to leave for the field.

Biblical and theological training. Mission agencies have historically required 30 semester hours (essentially one year) taken in an accredited institution. Denominational agencies will require more. If your church has exposed you to solid biblical and theological teaching, obvious through your testing, your training requirement may be less, depending on the agency.

Language learning (or language acquisition training) is a key skill to gain before leaving for the field, especially if learning languages has been difficult for you. Some agencies may require a semester of linguistics (the Summer Institute of Linguistics, SIL International, *www.sil.org*) or a language acquisition course (cf. COMPASS through Mission Training International, *http://mti.org/programs/ COMPASS*). If you can begin learning your future primary language before departure, it will accelerate your language learning and ministry goals upon arrival.

World Religions. You will likely be required to become familiar with the major world religion of your target people group (e.g. Islam, Buddhism, or Hinduism, as applicable).

Ministry experience. A strong relationship and ministry experience with your local church will probably fulfill most, if not all, of the agency's requirements for ministry experience.

Counseling. It is not uncommon for new appointees to have a prescribed number of personal or marriage counseling sessions, as appropriate and if needed.

Requirements unique to your particular field/team. Once you know the field team with which you'll be working, that team may require certain training before you can begin work with the team. Such requirements have often been developed after past new team members have encountered difficulty without such training in advance.

Support raising. If you're expected to raise you own support, you may be required to take special training in support raising. See the next step, *7. Get a support team!: Present your vision and raise up partners for prayer and financial support* for some pointers and resources that will get you going.

Support raising can be daunting! However, consider this:

All the skills required for support raising resemble skills required for church planting:

- Communication of intangible truth and vision;
- Meeting with strangers who you pray will become new friends;
- Depending completely on God for results;
- Trusting God to work in and through others; and
- Pulling committed people together into a partnership for ministry.

How long should training and support raising take?

After you've joined a mission agency, you will be expected to maintain a higher level of accountability and productivity with your time. Ideally the agency will provide a pre-field coach who will help you stay encouraged, motivated and accountable in your trek to the field. The agency's goal is to help you leave as soon as possible. More than likely your desire will be to leave even faster.

How much time will agency pre-field requirements take? It depends on your preparedness prior to application, the specific requirements of your agency, and the complexities of your prospective field assignment or work platform. If you and your church have done a great job in your training and affirming your call, the time needed to fulfill mission agency requirements will be greatly reduced.

Questions for reflection:

1. Sometimes missionaries feel that the choice of a mission agency is like a commitment to marriage: "till death do us part." Is that a good way to think about it?

2. What issues or events might cause you to leave a mission agency or to leave the mission field altogether?

3. How do you relate to those who have authority in your life? Do you respond with grace? Submission? Questioning? Resistance? Respect? How does factoring in the sovereignty of God help your attitude toward authority (cf. Romans 8:28)?

GET A SUPPORT TEAM!

Present your vision and raise up partners for prayer and financial support

At one mission agency's candidate orientation, a more mature couple that had been in their sending church for many years arrived with their support completely raised. It had taken a mere two months to complete the process. Others were amazed and asked them how they had been able to raise their support in such a short time frame. "Actually, it took 20 years," they said, referring to the fact that the relationships had been unknowingly cultivated long before it was time to begin support raising.

In contrast, a young woman missionary candidate of Indian descent was surprised by the strong reaction of her Christian parents to the process of "begging for money." They had strong family and cultural values of independence, self-respect, and receiving good pay for good work. They were totally unfamiliar with the "partnership development" model which funds most missions work. It was a huge shock to think that their precious daughter would be expected to raise her own support.

Both believing and unbelieving parents may raise objections to your desire to serve the Lord in challenging places so far away. Yet, the prospect of fund-raising is a lightning rod for resistance, even in your own heart! Be encouraged! Missionaries through the ages, from the Apostle Paul to the present, have cultivated financially supporting relationships; you can too.

Most likely you will be serving with a mission agency that requires you to raise both prayer and financial support. Some view this process as an unsavory task at first, but most look back at the process as a time when they discovered faith-stretching blessings and invaluable relationships along the way. Support raising has been a time-tested means of grace and supply for missionaries since the late 19th century.

Those who will serve with an agency that does not require personal support raising can still learn from the principles of communication and partnership in this section. Even when your salary, expenses, and benefits are underwritten through your agency, you still need to maintain a relationship of accountability and partnership with those who have invested in your life and ministry.

We've already noted how many of the activities and skills involved in church planting are involved in fund raising, or "partnership development." It's not too much to say that if you can't do the one, then you can't do the other.

Forty years ago when times were simpler and overseas costs were much lower, many missionaries raised their needed support in six months or less. Over the years that length of time has expanded. Though a long period of fundraising is not anyone's intention, it is not unusual to hear of missionary appointees taking 24-36 months in the partnership development phase. The time of transition between regular employment (or school) and full-time field missionary is often difficult. Mission agencies are less willing to endure appointees raising support over some indefinite extended period of times. They tend more toward tighter accountability and deadlines for support raising. Failure to meet specific activity goals and major deadlines may result in loss of membership in the agency.

Three major figures in missions history represent three distinct approaches to the fundraising process.

- D.L. Moody prayed, informed people of needs, and asked for funds directly.
- J. Hudson Taylor prayed and informed people of needs.
- George Muller prayed.

God has historically supplied the needs of people who have used each of these methods. Perhaps you are inclined to one of these approaches. You may need to ask God how He would have you approach the process. Regardless of the method, let's examine important principles to remember in the fundraising process.

- **Partnership development (support raising) is a part of your ministry**, rather than a necessary evil that precedes your ministry. You have an important discipleship relationship with your supporters. They exercise generous stewardship of spiritual and material resources to enable your ministry; you exercise visionary spiritual leadership toward them. They become World Christian participants in the Great Commission through you. This was true even in the 1st century:

> Partnership development (support raising) is a part of your ministry.
>
> God is your ultimate source of support.
>
> Relationships are foundational in support raising.
>
> Communication is key.

And you Philippians yourselves know that in the beginning of the gospel, when I left Macedonia, no church entered into partnership with me in giving and receiving, except you only. Even in Thessalonica you sent me help for my needs once and again. Not that I seek the gift, but I seek the fruit that increases to your credit.

(Philippians 4:15-17)

Beloved, it is a faithful thing you do in all your efforts for these brothers, strangers as they are, who testified to your love before the church. You will do well to send them on their journey in a manner worthy of God. For they have gone out for the sake of the name, accepting nothing from the Gentiles. Therefore we ought to support people like these, that we may be fellow workers for the truth.

(3 John 1:5-8)

- **God is your ultimate source of support.** Inevitably some people and churches whom you feel sure will support you, will not. And individuals and churches you believe will not support you, will. If you understand that all of your support comes from God, then you'll be free to communicate broadly, confidently, and passionately about His desire to be glorified in all nations. Let God do His work in the hearts and checkbooks of your prospective supporters. You do your part in communicating your vision for your part of the Great Commission well. By God's grace, He will supply your support needs. The common key to each of those three support raising models is an abundant quantity and quality of communication.

- **Relationships are foundational in support raising**, as described in this unit's opening story. This need not mean that everyone you approach for support must be an intimate friend. It does mean that usually some level of relationship must be present, or develop, in the fundraising process.

- **Communication is key.** Tailor your communication and appeal to your audience. Important to effective communication are the following:
  - Clarity of vision and goals
  - The more personal, the better
  - Frequency and repetition of key points
  - Warmth and rapport
  - Real-life testimonials and anecdotes
  - Specific data and action points
  - Visual elements complement and enhance verbal and written elements

Getting started

How do you develop your initial "mailing list" (while acknowledging that email and web-based media is becoming the standard)? Consider these categories.

- Your "Christmas card" friends
- Your parents' ministry contacts, if applicable
- Fellow believers from your university
- Your church family (if allowed by your church's policies)
- Your ministry contacts and those discipled by you
- Your small group Bible study
- Christian business associates
- Your past or present community teams or clubs
- Churches in your home church's network, fellowship, or denomination
- Mission agency contacts in your area

- Churches committed to reaching Unreached People Groups (UPGs)
- Churches committed to reaching your target country
- Churches committed to reaching your target people group
- Christian nationals from your target country
- People with whom you have served in ministry

Secure third party endorsements and participation in the process. For example, a letter from your pastor to other like-minded pastors or pastors' fellowships in your area is usually helpful. People in your small group can write and design elements of your presentation, or assemble promotional packets for distribution. You may have friends who can help you create or improve aspects of your media presentations, including PowerPoint, displays, graphic design and layout, video, photography, blogs, brochures, newsletters, email distribution and phone contacts.

How long should this support raising process take?

Like many projects, your results tend to correlate with the amount of time and effort you invest. In God's providence, some people will be better resourced to raise support quickly. For example, your parents may have been involved in Christian ministry throughout your lifetime; as such, their friends and colleagues in ministry will be more inclined to support you. On the other hand, if you became a believer during your college years and haven't been integrally involved in a solid local church, you can expect to take more time to achieve 100% support.

If you are able to devote full time to partnership development and if you have tangible assistance from others for support raising, you should expect to spend 6-12 months in the process. Putting thoughtful and creative work into developing excellent materials and presentations before you begin the fundraising process will help tremendously.

If you are not able to devote full time to partnership development and if you do not have tangible assistance from others, you may be among those spending 24-36 months in the process.

Get to work! You absolutely should not expect bags of money to fall from heaven. But if that does happen, give God all the glory (it's not because you are so special). You pray. You do the part for which you are responsible. God will do His work in ways exceedingly, abundantly beyond all you could ask or think (Ephesians 3:20-21).

Did you know that Jesus was supported?

Questions for reflection:

1. What words describe your attitude about support raising?

2. Research how ministry was supported in the New Testament? e.g. – Did you know that Jesus was supported? (see Luke 8:1-3)

Resources:

Your agency may recommend a missionary support-raising seminar. There are a number of books and video resources available. We recommend: *Funding Your Ministry*, by Scott Morton (Dawson Media, 1999).

TntMPD® Powerful software for ministry partner development is highly recommended and can be found for free at *www.TNTware.com*

Building a supportive team around you from your home church is of incalculable help and encouragement along the way. They become adjunct staff to you in your support raising, and more! Three easily accessible resources are:

- Neil Pirolo's book, *Serving As Senders*. This is an excellent guide to creating a "sending team" that will help you in support development, as one of six key areas of support throughout your missionary career.
- Also, Bethlehem Baptist Church of Minneapolis, MN, has some solid materials available online for launching a "Barnabas Team." Do a search for "Barnabas Support Teams" at *www.hopeinGod.org*
- Do a search for "Barnabas Team" and look for downloadable PDFs at *www.Propempo.com*

Betty Barnett, *Friend Raising* (YWAM Publishing, 2002)

William Dillon, *People Raising* (Moody Publishers, 2012)

Paul Johnson, *More Than Money, More Than Faith*
(Pleasant Word, 2007)

Steve Shadrach, *The God Ask*, (CMM Press, 2013)

The most recognized non-agency-specific training for faith support raising is the *Support Raising Bootcamp*, conducted by Support Raising Solutions. Go to:
www.supportraisingsolutions.org/bootcamp

GET OVER THERE!

Get your church to celebrate and send you out

In the film *Mr. Holland's Opus*, Mr. Holland, a beloved music faculty member at a local high school, is forced to retire from a thirty-year career due to budget cuts. For years he's poured his life into helping students love music who otherwise would not have. In the process, they've gained skills that they've used in other walks of life. The film ends with a surprise going-away assembly, where current students form the audience, and alumni on stage are ready to play under Mr. Holland's direction. He is handed the baton and given the opportunity to direct the orchestra playing an *opus* that he's quietly been writing. And with a tearful but celebratory event, Mr. Holland moves on to his next phase of life amidst loud and appreciative cheering.

Finally it's time to depart for the field. A celebratory send off (not very different from Mr. Holland's!) is appropriate. While you are being sent, it's the product of many supporters, friends, prayer warriors, encouragers, donors, mentors, advisors, trainers and helpers who have sacrificially given to make this possible. They have been working together almost as a symphony to make it possible. Almost nothing is more exciting and energizing to the spiritual life of a local church than the sending out (cf. 3 John 5-8, "propempo"-ing) of its own sons and daughters into strategic roles fulfilling the Great Commission.

Part of the celebration includes, Lord willing, the fact that your sending church has been involved in every step of your path to the field, from your commitment at CROSS, through your preparation, to God's supply to send you out THERE. The occasion of recognizing the completion of your readiness and setting you apart for missionary service makes the congregation feel as though they are all crossing the finish line together with you, as you continue your quest for Christ's glory among the nations. Christ is worthy! It's because of Him and for Him that this is possible.

What follows below are some simple ideas for elements of a formal commissioning service. It has much the same sense of solemn celebration found in a pastoral ordination service. Not all of these elements may fit your church's ethos and traditions. And not all possibilities for the service are listed below.

- The biblical basis for sending missionaries (cf. Acts 13:3)
- A printed program that includes ways to contact the new missionary, and security guidelines for communication, if necessary
- Invitations issued to church leaders, church members, a representative of the mission agency, family members of the missionary, donors and prayer partners
- Worship, including music appropriate to missions and commitment
- Scripture reading
- The missionary's testimony of salvation and calling
- An interview with the missionary regarding the preparation process, vision for ministry on the field and ministry goals
- Recognition of those who have played particularly significant roles in the missionary's qualification process: mentors, prayer partners, etc.
- A biblical charge to the missionary, usually a short message from the senior/preaching pastor to the missionary
- A word of commendation or testimony from the mission agency representative

- Recognition of the Barnabas Team, who will stand behind the missionary with practical personal support
- An explanation of the preparation and qualification process, usually by a church leader or Missions Team leader
- A charge to the congregation
- A prayer of dedication
- A response or acceptance of the charge by the missionary
- The presentation of a commissioning certificate
- A reception following the event

Questions for reflection:

1. Whom should you personally thank for their prayers, advocacy, help, encouragement, or partnership with you in the process before you leave for your mission field?

2. Carve out some special private time just to praise and thank God for His great grace to enable and allow you to arrive at this launching point of your ministry.

POSTLOGUE

What if it doesn't work out? What if I don't end up making it to the mission field?

You thought you were called to go to the mission field. You hoped and prayed and planned to take the Gospel for the glory of Christ to an unreached people group. A variety of reasons and circumstances have now combined to make this unlikely or impossible, at least for now. This shouldn't mean abandoning missions involvement altogether.

What should your next steps be?

First, understand that you are not alone. Many intend to go, but estimates tell us that only about 15% of those who plan to go actually arrive on the field. Intending to go is not a bad thing. Through your passion and heart for missions, you've learned a lot. You've grown in spiritual maturity and skill in the process.

Second, know that God's call still stands, though probably not in the same way you thought at the beginning of this process. Maybe you understand more clearly now that following hard after God does not guarantee you a particular slot or role. He obviously intended that you head in that direction for specific purposes in your life and in His plan for others, ultimately for His glory. He always lovingly, graciously, tenaciously calls you to love Christ, to grow to be more like Him, to share Him wherever you are. He calls you to godliness and service and worship, just as much now as ever.

Third, you are not a failure because you didn't make it to the field. If you were humble and teachable in the process, God will still use all of it for His glory in your life. Your education will help you and others down the road. God uses everything in our lives as a prologue for what He intends for us to do. There is no "second best" in God's will. Your inability to make it to the field did not come as a surprise to God, nor will it catch Him shorthanded. If you did not sin in the process, you did not somehow let God down. His purposes for you are good and acceptable and perfect. You may have been humbled; you may have to change direction; but you are not a failure.

> There is no "second best" in God's will. Your NOT making it to the field is no surprise to God. His purposes for you are good and acceptable and perfect. You may have been humbled; but you are not a failure.

Fourth, you have become a seasoned "World Christian." You are in an excellent position to play a different role in missions. You understand more about missions and the process of becoming a missionary than ever before. You are convinced of the importance of the local church in the process. You know about the personal, spiritual, and material costs of going THERE. Let this mark you life! Don't quench your passion for world missions. Express it and channel it in different ways, including:

- Praying for the unreached, and facilitating others to pray regularly for missions
- Giving generously to missions
- Encouraging and mobilizing others to be a part of God's heart for the nations

- Caring for missionaries on the field, ideally with others In a "Barnabas Team" context (see Neal Pirolo's *Serving as Senders* book)
- Mobilizing your church for missions by starting or joining your church's missions team
- Mentoring new missionary candidates
- Welcoming the nations by reaching out cross-culturally in your city

Lastly, don't blame God. We can mix up God's call and our own desires. God is neither at fault nor mistaken in your change of intended direction. God's purposes are still pure and good. Talk to God about this unanticipated diversion. Express your emotions, but don't blame God; don't become bitter and resentful. He is sovereign; you are not. He is all loving, kind, gracious, forgiving, and full of integrity. He wants you to pray. He entreats you to approach His throne of mercy. To learn His compassion for you and get a bearing on new direction, spend extra time in His Word. Seek godly counsel, not an audience for your grievances. Try to figure out what new path He is setting before you **HERE**. Set new goals. Actively seek to serve. Press on!

APPENDIX A
Practical guidelines for security concerns

Quick Dos and Don'ts

1. Do communicate widely and enthusiastically about your desire to serve the Lord and take the Gospel to the unreached.
2. Don't say, write or post anything publicly that specifically labels you as a "missionary" or identifies your specific chosen target people group.
3. Do read and research the current culture, politics and religious environment of the group you hope to reach.
4. Don't become afraid or paranoid about your prospective status and situation THERE.
5. Do take balanced, wise and reasonable precautions in preparation for security and contingency concerns (specialized security training, appropriate security devices and practices, legal documents like wills and power of attorney, etc.).
6. Don't go overboard and spend too much time and money trying to prevent every possible risk and contingency.

Description of Communication Restriction Levels

A brief overview of security guidelines adapted from Pioneers:

Non-restricted: Communication to and from the team can remain completely open without particular restrictions on vocabulary or terms.

- No problem using the "company" name "PIONEERS."
- No problem using Christian or missionary terminology.
- No problem communicating confidential materials.

Low: Communication with the team may remain open. Still, exercise discretion with "company" name, internal terminology, and confidential material.

- Do not use the "company" name
- Use discretion when communicating confidential information
- Use discretion when using Christian, ministry, or missions terms

Moderate: Communication with the team must not include obvious words that describe the missionary role or ministry. Communicate with innuendo, euphemisms and "coded" messages only. Assume unfriendly groups are monitoring communications.

- Do not use the "company" name.
- At this level encrypted, secure email is a must.
- Encrypted computer drives, sectors, memory, and back-up are a must.

High: Communication to the team must not include obvious or coded words regarding missionaries' roles and ministries.

- Foreign governments almost certainly are monitoring the communication.
- All messages must only be about non-ministry related material and still remain vague in content.
- Do not use the "company" name.
- Do not make direct references to connections with other workers in communication, if possible.

Do not Contact: Communication with the team is not allowed due to an extreme security risk. Team members will be responsible to initiate contact with people outside of their country.

APPENDIX B
Sample My Sending Church / Mission Agency Partnership Agreement

SUPPORTING PARTNERSHIP AGREEMENT (simplified)

Partnership Purpose Statement:

The "My Sending Church" (MSC) – "The Mission Agency" partnership exists to jointly support a church planting team or team members to a selected, unreached people group area so that God will be glorified as Christ builds indigenous, multiplying churches among them.

The partnership will establish the terms of cooperation in the context of ministry focused on target group/area and guiding and supporting the ministry teams.

Partnership Roles:

Issues	My Sending Church (MSC)	The Mission Agency
Policy	Accepts and approves The Mission Agency policies and/or guidelines	Provides policies and/or guidelines
Selecting Team Members	Identifies, pre-screens, trains, and/or otherwise selects personnel for the Project Team Sends MSC-approved candidates to The Mission Agency as appointees Commits to spiritual, pastoral, and provide some financial support for those approved.	Provides MSC with pre-field preparation requirements. Processes and assesses candidate for acceptance to The Mission Agency membership. Agrees to allow MSC equivalent examination in place of psychological testing and counseling.

Supervision	MSC is prepared to assume significant responsibility for spiritual and pastoral care and counsel for all members of the Project Team. Cooperates with The Mission Agency administration of the church planter's field activities to The Mission Agency.	US office and field leaders provide regular administrative supervision, pastoral care and counsel for the Project Team on field assignment. Provides MSC with all information relevant to the care and nurture of the personnel on the field.
Financial Responsibility	Commits to provide financial support for the church planter, sourced from both inside and outside the church. Assists church planter in procurement of personal and ministry support as established by The Mission Agency. MSC will shepherd and track the progress of the support raising process.	Establishes annual plans and budgets with the church planting team. Accepts and approves annual field activity reports. Manages all funds received for the church planter's personal needs and ministry, salary, medical, retirement, reimbursement of ministry expenses, etc.
Building the Relationship	Appoint a partnership coordinator to facilitate communication and monitor the partnership relationship.	Appoint a partnership coordinator to facilitate communication and monitor the partnership relationship.
Role of the Partnership Coordinator	Serves as the primary contact person. Coordinates home assignment visits by the church planter.	Serves as primary contact person. Facilitates communication regarding ministry progress and support status.

Termination of the Agreement:

Every reasonable good faith effort should be made to implement the terms of this agreement or modify it to be of mutual value to all those involved. However, if this agreement is not achieving its intended objectives, and after mutual communication and response has been exchanged toward restoration of its value and/or effectiveness, this agreement may be terminated at the request of either party.

Signed:

APPENDIX C
21 Questions for Missionary Candidates

Please circle Y for "Yes" or N for "No" beside each item below. Then, sign the page.

Policy on Candidate Responses: You are expected to answer all issues raised with highest integrity and honesty. Your responses must not intentionally or consciously mislead, misrepresent the truth, or omit any relevant information. A "Yes" answer does not necessarily disqualify you for service. However, you will be expected to give further information and/or clarification for any items answered "Yes."

Please consider each item as beginning with the words: "Do you now have any involvement with or have you ever participated in or experienced..."

Sexual Health Issues

Y N   sexual immorality, including emotional infidelity.

Y N   homosexuality, including temptation and thought life.

Y N   pornography, including all types, sources, and media.

Y N   child molestation or child sexual enticement, sexual assault or sexual harassment.

Y N   repetitive, abnormal, unusual, or inappropriate sexual fantasizing or masturbation.

Medical Health Issues

Y N   prolonged use of (a) prescription drug(s).

Y N   substance abuse of any kind.

Y N surgery and/or hospitalization (except for births).

Y N communicable, or life-threatening disease.

Y N extended medical, naturist, chiropractic, psychological, or psychiatric care.

Y N a history of medical trauma, repeated history of a particular illness or of broken bones.

Y N stress related illness, including but not limited to severe headaches, nausea and vomiting, hives, skin rashes, diarrhea or incontinence, hypertensive responses (e.g. hyperventilating), partial and/or temporary paralysis.

Y N seizure/s, stroke/s, amnesia, or significant mental lapse.

Mental, Emotional and Psychological Health Issues

Y N extended counseling, psychological, or psychiatric care.

Y N antidepressant, stimulant, or mood-enhancing drugs, whether prescribed or over-the-counter.

Y N extended use of weight loss products, tendencies to any food disorders.

Y N a history of depression, anti-social behavior, histrionics, rage, anger, violence, or uncontrolled emotional outbursts.

Y N self-inflicted harm of any type or suicidal tendencies.

Y N inappropriate, abnormal, or unusual reaction/s to stress.

Y N inappropriate, abnormal, or unusual family relationships.

Is there anything else in your personal life or history which, upon discovery and review by godly leaders using commonly understood biblical principles, virtues, and ethics, might be viewed as detrimental to the testimony and reputation of your ministry and/or that of your church and mission?

APPENDIX D:
Why "church planting" is
THE priority ministry in missions

When the modern missionary candidate thinks of missions around the world, he/she is drawn to consider genuine, desperate human needs. We think of many solutions to those needs that seem so accessible for us to offer to the needy world, including:

Well-drilling
Water supply projects
Medical clinics
Prevention of human trafficking
Sports evangelism
Mass evangelism meetings
Community development
AIDS-related programs
Bible translation
Agricultural development
Internet evangelism
Cottage industry development
Teaching English
Computer/IT training
Electrical supply projects
Reforestation projects
Dental clinics
Sports training clinics
Orphan care
Aquaculture
Building or construction
Youth ministry and camps
Poverty alleviation
Primary health care
Expatriate services

Special skills development
Carpentry
Cabinet-making
Plumbing
Welding
Auto mechanics
Peddle-taxi, motorbike taxi
Embroidery
Garment making
Jewelry making
Weaving
Carpet making
Pottery
Wood carving
Sculpturing
Art
"Business As Mission"
Business skills development
NGO service
Micro-loan projects
VBS or Bible clubs
Music ministry
Disaster relief & development
Adoption services

Yet the greatest human need is for the Gospel. "I was obsessed with the issues of justice and human trafficking until I came to reckon with the ultimate injustice: folks who've never had a chance to hear the gospel," said a candidate at one mission agency's recent candidate orientation.

We should rightly be appalled by the deplorable circumstances and injustices that evidence a fallen world. We are appropriately gripped by catastrophic human needs, sometimes with life and death hanging in the balance. But it's easy to believe that those presenting symptoms must take precedence. In some cases, they must. The spiritually lost may need to be rescued from death in order to even have a chance to hear to Gospel. Still, we can confuse "means" with "ends"; we mix up "strategies" with "results." Our desire for holistic transformation of life and society can eclipse a clear biblical ambition for proclamation of the Gospel.

Missions strategies that do not intentionally start, sustain and multiply indigenous local churches fall short of the biblical ideal. Projects that began as an entrée into or point of contact in the community in order to share the gospel very easily became ends in themselves. Sometimes a concerned outside observer can help a missionary avoid this trap. Again, your relationship with an involved sending church can help at this point. Disciple making is the core of the Great Commission. Great Commission-driven disciple making will naturally result in local churches. The baptizing, teaching and obeying of "all I commanded you" takes place in the context of a mutually committed and worshiping body of believers. That is clearly what the first-century believers understood and did; they were the original recipients of the Great Commission. Planting churches is how they obeyed it.

Discipling whole nations (people groups) must include gathering new disciples into self-supporting, self-governing, self-propagating bodies of believers. This is critical for a number of reasons. Indigenous churches corporately portray Christ to a watching world in credible, culturally appropriate ways—something impossible for cultural outsiders to do. They demonstrate lives committed to the "one another" commands of Scripture. Local churches stay when foreign missionaries cannot. Local churches persist when persecution mounts. Local churches express the Gospel and transformational biblical truth in ways no other non-church ministry can.

The many ministries listed at this appendix's opening are good and legitimate means to the end of establishing indigenous local churches. These strategies should ultimately build bridges, establish relationships, open opportunities, and facilitate the goal of planting churches. Indigenous local churches are the God-ordained instruments for each people group reaching and discipling its own people group.

Jesus said, "*I will build My church.*" Matt. 16:18

Paul wrote, "*Christ loved the church and gave Himself up for her.*" Eph. 5:25

Paul also writes, "*through the church the manifold wisdom of God might now be made known … This was according to the eternal purpose that he has realized in Christ Jesus our Lord*" Eph. 3:10-11

And, "*to him be glory in the church and in Christ Jesus throughout all generations, forever and ever. Amen.*" Eph. 3:21

Personal Progress Trail Journal

Personal Progress Trail Journal

Personal Progress Trail Journal

Personal Progress Trail Journal

Personal Progress Trail Journal

Personal Progress Trail Journal